Francis Henry Appleton

Historical Extracts

Peabody Institute

Francis Henry Appleton

Historical Extracts
Peabody Institute

ISBN/EAN: 9783337395179

Printed in Europe, USA, Canada, Australia, Japan

Cover: Foto ©ninafisch / pixelio.de

More available books at **www.hansebooks.com**

Peabody Institute of Peabody,
Mass., U.S.A..

Historical " Extracts

from
The Memorial Volume
published in 1856,

and from
The Thirty Seven Annual Reports
of the
Board of Trustees.
to date.

1890.

The Compiler of these Historical Extracts has, literally, only done what is stated on the front page of this collection. He has used the original wording as far as possible, and has done so in the hope that these, who are not familiar with the history of our splendid Institution, and its contents, will be induced to read this condensed record, and learn of it, how much we are indebted to the noble founder, and those who have aided him under in his good work.

F. H. A.

1890.

It seems appropriate to present, for the Some account of the origin of the Peabody Institute, as prefatory to submitting the following extracts from the 37 Annual Reports which have, with their accompanying reports of the Sub-committees, been presented to date of the Board of Trustees; and for that purpose statements and records, contained in the Memorial Volume published in 1856, are drawn upon, and used thereafter.

The citizens of the original Town of Danvers (now Danvers and Peabody) had determined to celebrate the one hundredth anniversary of the existence of the town as a distinct municipal corporation, which fell upon Wednesday, the 16 June 1852. Although Mr Peabody had long been absent, yet the many proofs by which he had, in previous instances, evinced his regard for the place of his birth, gave him peculiar claims to be included among the invited guests. Accordingly, an invitation was early forwarded to him, by the Committee of the Town, to be present at that festival, with a request that, if unable to attend, he would dignify by letter his interest in the occasion. In his reply, after stating that his engagements would allow him to comply only with the latter part of the request, he said, "I enclose a sentiment which I ask may remain sealed till this letter is read on the day of celebration, according to the direction on the envelope."

The endorsement on the envelope of the sealed packet was as follows:—

"The seal of this is not to be broken till the toasts are being proposed by the Chairman, at the dinner, 16th. June, at Danvers, in commemoration of the one hundredth year since its deliverance from Salem. It contains a sentiment for the occasion, from George Peabody, of London."

In obedience to the above direction, at the proper moment the reading of the communication was called for; and the following was received by the delighted audience with loud acclamations:—

"By George Peabody, of London:—

"Education — A debt due from present to future generations."

In his letter, which was read Mr. Peabody made known his first gift of "#20000.," for the promotion of knowledge and morality among "~~~~~~" the inhabitants of Danvers. He says "the conditions are that the legal voters of the town, at a meeting to be held at a convenient time after the 16th. June, shall accept the gift, and shall elect a Committee, of not less than twelve persons, to receive and have charge of the same, for the purpose of establishing a Lyceum for the delivery of lectures upon such subjects as may be designated by a Committee of the town, free to all the inhabitants. under such rules as said Committee may from time to time enact; and that a Library shall be obtained, which shall also be free to the inhabitants, under the direction of the Committee.

"That a suitable building for the use of the Lyceum shall be erected, at a cost, including land, fixtures, furniture, &c., not exceeding seven thousand dollars, and shall be located within one-third of a mile of the Presbyterian Meeting House, occupying the spot of that formerly under the pastoral care of the Rev. Mr. Walker, in the south parish of Danvers.

"That ten thousand dollars of this gift shall be invested by the town's Committee, in undoubted securities, as a permanent fund, the interest arising therefrom to be expended in support of the Lyceum.

"In other respects, I leave the disposition of the affairs of the Lyceum to the inhabitants of Danvers, — merely suggesting that it might be advisable for them, by their own act, to exclude sectarian theology and political discussions forever from the walls of the institution."

At Town Meeting held 28 June 1852, the Communication from Mr. Peabody was read by the Moderator, and appropriate resolves were passed upon motion of Mr. Andrew Nichols. And a Board of twelve Trustees was chosen.

The proceedings of the town, having been transmitted to Mr. Peabody, received his approval. The officers of the Institute, therefore, are a Board of Trustees chosen by the town, in whom are vested its funds and other property, for the purpose of maintaining a Lyceum and Library; and another Board, chosen annually by the Trustees, called the Lyceum and Library Committee, whose duties are to superintend and direct all its active operations. (These last two sentences are copied from the Memorial Volume published in 1856.)

[Mr. Peabody was made familiar with the Rules and Regulations as adopted in 1857, which, appearing to have, provoked no unfavorable comment from him.]

16 June 1852 –	Mr. Peabody gives $20000.
	($10000. for a permanent fund.)
1852.	Mr. Peabody also gives $10000. additional.
20 aug. 1853.	Corner Stone of building laid.
28 Sept. 1854.	Mr. Peabody's portrait rec'd. & placed in Hall
29 Sept. 1854.	Dedication of building. Address by Rufus Cho
18 Oct. 1854.	Library opened with about 5000 volum
18 May 1855.	Town of South Danvers incorporated.
9 Oct. 1856.	Public Reception in honor of Mr. Peabody.
1856 – 1857.	$20000. from Mr. Peabody he holding the
" "	$10000. to Danvers from Mr. Peabody.
" "	$15000. from Mr. Peabody to purchase Mason
	and Sutton Estates.
" "	$1500. from Mr. Peabody to move Mason
	house and build wall and fence
" "	$1100. to pay all liabilities outs
1857 – 1858.	Mr. Peabody's bust, by J. S. Jones, and Grand Pia
	given by him.
1858 – 1859.	Portrait of Pres't. Harrison given by Mr. S. W. Up
" "	" " Genl. Gideon Pierce " " "
1859 – 1860	" " Rufus Choate " " "
1862 – 1863	" " Edward Everett " "
1863 – 1864	Gold Box, with the Freedom of City of London
" "	Found Centennial Parish of Chelsea &
" "	Elk Horns and Minerals given by Thomas
" "	10000 volumes in library.
July 1866	Mr. Peabody's visit to the Institute
" "	" " gift of $100000. " " "
" "	" " " " $20000. to Danvers.
22 Sept. "	Queen's portrait and autograph letter receive
15 Oct. "	Mrs. Sutton's gift of $20000.
1867 – 1868.	Enlargement of Building; Strong Room and Portico he
5 aug. 1867.	Mr. Peabody gives $2000. for High School Medal
1868 · 1869.	Congressional Medal given
" "	Engravings of Ancient & Modern Jerusalem given by

Sept. 1868.	Mr. Peabody visits America & gives $50000
Sept. 1869.	Reserved Fund established
69-1870.	Mr. Peabody's sickness and death at London; imposing funeral ceremonies in England and in his native country and town
Sept. 1872.	New Catalogue prepared.
72-1873.	Hammond House bought for Reserve Fund
" "	Mr. Fitch Poole, Librarian, died.
77-1878.	Copy of "Civil War Shield" given by Mrs. Lind
" "	18000 volumes in library.
" "	Death of Eben S. Osborne, leaving will giving ½ interest in his property to Sutton Library at death of his widow. Will dated 30 May 1877. E. W. Jacobs and D. Webster King, Trustees.
79-1880.	Gold Medal and Diploma from Peabody Education Fund deposited.
82-1883.	23 271 volumes in library.
ober 1884.	Hon. Alfred A. Abbott died.
mary 1887.	Heirs of Mr. Peabody established a Fund of $1000., income for Peabody Room Lot
June 1887.	Library to be open every day.

Other gifts.

Autograph letters of Earl Russell and Sir James Emerson Tennant.

Gold Box presented to Mr. Peabody by the Fishmongers of London.

Framed memorial from Workingmen of London.

" " " Merchant Tailors of London

Portfolio of Photographic likenesses of the Queen and members of the Royal Family.

1st. Annual Report,
(1852 – 1853.)

6 June 1852. Notice of Mr. Peabody's intention to donate money for the Institute was
received. In a letter, dated 23 July, from
Mr. Peabody, was enclosed a draft for $20,000.
on bankers. Blake, Ward & Co., Boston, which was
loaned at 6%. Later he sent an additional
$10000. donation.

A lot of land was purchased from Eben
Sutton, Esq., being the Westerly part of what
was then the Dennison Wallis Estate – 70 feet on
Main St., & extending back 110 feet, with
rights of way, 16 ft wide on westerly side and 20
feet in the rear. Price $3000.; with the use
of 25 feet more land in rear to be used in common
with Mr. Sutton for $100. more.

Refusal of the whole Wallis estate for
$6500., measuring about 135 feet on Main St,
and 160 feet from front to rear, with brick
dwelling and barn.

The corner stone was laid on August 20, 1853,
the weather being exceedingly favorable and a
vast number of people were present. The
exercises commenced at 4: P.M. under direction
the President of the Board of Trustees, Hon. Robert
Daniels, the Committee and guests occupying a
raised platform, with the band of music in
attendance.
After a brief address by Mr. Daniels, the
Rev. Milton P. Braman offered prayer.
An address following by Hon. Alfred A.
Abbott. Hon. Abbott Lawrence, at Mr. Peabody's
request as well as at the earnest request of the
trustees, addressed the assemblage and then

laid the corner stone at the north-
west angle of the Building.

Addresses were also made by Hon. Benjamin
Seaver, Mayor of Boston; Hon. Asahel Hunt-
ington, Mayor of Salem; Hon. George S.
Hillard, of Boston & Hon. Charles W. Upham,
of Salem.

Full reports of the speeches can be
found appended to the Volume published
in 1856, containing an account of the
reception and dinner to Mr. Peabody on
October 6th. of that year.

2nd. Annual Report,
(1853 - 1854.)

About 2000 books, already purchased, and
most all on the shelves. $3000. was appropriated for the library.
10 April 1854, Building nearly done.
It was built by Russell and Whit of
Salem, and Franklin A. Merrill of Danvers,
with Mr. Bond as Architect.

The furnishing of the Hall, and
building the fence, only, now remain.

3d. Annual Report.
(1854 - 1855.)

29 September 1854, Building completed and dedicated. Mr. Rufus Choate appeared among his former Townsmen and delivered the address. ~~moderate~~ Library opened to the public 18 October 1854. 2500 volumes have been received from Mrs. Peabody, making total volumes about 5000. ~~Remarks for $2000~~ A 6 of the dedication ceremonies is contained in the Memorial Volume published in 1856.

Mr. E. B. Hinckley, instructor in Peabody High School in attendance, as librarian, Wednesdays and Saturdays from 8 to 10 P.M.

Free course of eleven lectures; also a course of seven lectures to which tickets were sold.

In making choice of books, applicants are allowed to consult them on the shelves.

At Town meeting Feby. 1854, it was voted to request Mr. Peabody to give his full length portrait, which he did and it was placed in position the day before the dedication. ~~To all painted by~~ ~~Healy.~~

(1855–1856.)

The first Catalogue was printed in 1855.

The affairs of the Institute are formally reported upon.

By an Act of the Legislature, passed 18 May 1855, that part of the town of Danvers in which the Peabody Institute is ~~located~~ located, was incorporated as a new town by the name of South Danvers.

Mr. Peabody presented ~~also~~ a grand piano and his Marble Bust to the Institute.

On 21 August 1856 a legal public meeting was held upon petition of the Trustees to take the necessary steps to arrange for a public Reception and Dinner to Mr. Peabody upon the occasion of his visit to his native Country and Town. Resolutions were adopted and a Committee of twenty three gentlemen was appointed.

The Resolutions being sent to the Town of Danvers, similar action was taken there and a Committee of twenty one was appointed.

These Committees meet together and organized jointly. Delegations from each met Mr. Peabody upon his arrival in New York, and extended their invitation to him.

Similar invitations were presented to him from several large Cities but he declined all except that from his native Town.

The joint Committee therefore decided that their demonstration "should have something of the character of internationality."

The British Consul at Boston was present as well as other representatives of the United Kingdom, and "the Stars and Stripes waved in amity with the cross of St. George."

The day opened with beautiful weather. Mr. Peabody arrived at Danvers, at about 10 o'clock; and was escorted, led by a mounted band, by a Cavalcade composed of Ladies and gentlemen, from the meeting place on Maple Street, beneath numerous triumphal arches and under waving flags, through Streets lined with decorated houses, attended by the booming of cannon and strains of martial music, with the shouts and salutations of the people. The route was by the most direct route through Davenport, to the head of Central Street, where the several bodies composing the procession were drawn up to receive him. It consisted of the Town Authorities, the Schools, the members of the Fire Departments, strangers from abroad, and our own citizens, and some other organizations. The Divisionary Corps of Cadets, under Captain Foster, performed escort duty with Gilmore's Band. General Wm. Sutton was Chief Marshal.

The procession moved through Central and Main Streets to the Salem boundary line, countermarched to Holten Street, through Holten, and returned by Washington and Main Streets to the Institute Building, where the address was delivered by Hon. Alfred [?], following an address by Rev. [?]. After the exercises at the Institute, a new procession was formed, consisting of holders of tickets to the dinner, and the Schools, who proceeded to the tables under military escort. The route was through Washington Street to the lot of land

upon which J. B. Smith's large Pavilion had been erected with accommodation for 1500 guests.

Hon. Robert S. Daniels presided and Rev. Mr. Murray was introduced a Chaplain,

Mr. Peabody addressed the assemblage, and was followed by Governor Gardner, Hon. Edward Everett, Mr. J. B. C. Davis of New York, President Walker of Harvard College, Hon. Wm. S. Messervy, Mayor of Salem, Prof. C. C. Felton, Mr. Charles Hale of Boston, Hon. G. W. Warren, Ex-Mayor of Charlestown, Hon. Otis P. Lord of Salem, Judge White, Judge Upham of New Hampshire, Mrs. Carruthers of England and Hon. Charles W. Upham of Salem. A song by Mr. J. R. Peabody was sung by a Glee Club, to the tune of Auld Lang Syne; an Ode by Mrs. George A. Osborne, was sung to the tune of America; and finally an Ode by Harriet W. Preston, also to the tune of Auld Lang Syne.

At the conclusion of these exercises Mr. Peabody was escorted to Mr. Daniels residence, where he passed the night.

In the evening a Levee was held at the Hall of the Institute where Mr. Peabody received the citizens of the town. Mr. Daniels and General Wm. Sutton also held receptions the same evening, both of which Mr. Peabody attended.

The next day Mr. Peabody visited the Institute, inspected the books and methods used in the management of the library, and examined the Treasurer's books. He later visited the "homes and haunts" and friends of his youth, and at five o'clock started for Georgetown, passing through

(1856 – 1857.) continued –

~~Reception to Mr. Peabody~~ 9 October 1856

Mr. Peabody established an additional
fund of #20000., the principal to remain
in his own hands, the interest to be
paid demi-annually during his life, and
the report says "may be considered a
donation of #20000..

#10000. was given at same time to
found a library at Danvers, with Mr.
Mr Nathaniel Hills as librarian–

#15000. also given to purchase Sutton
and Merrill Estates and improve
grounds by Mr. Peabody; together
with an amount of #1500. to pay
for moving Merrill house, and building
wall and fence on westerly side of
the grounds.

Previous to Mr Peabody's departure
for Europe he made an additional
gift of #1100. to pay off all
liabilities against the Institute

6th Annual Report,
(1857 - 1858.)

Income as reported at close of year is:-

6% on $10000. permanent fund	600.
6% on 20000. held by Mr. Peabody	1200.
income from real estate	500.
Total -	$2300.

There are about 6000 volumes in library with Mrs. Fitch Poole as librarian.

By the By-laws adopted early in this year nearly all the active, direction and control of affairs of the Institute devolves upon the Lyceum and Library Committee. They have the entire charge of the Library and the course of Lectures, and the appropriation and disbursements of all the income of the funds of the Institute as the same, year by year, is passed to their credit and submitted to their use by the Trustees.

This year the amounts so appropriated were $600. for the Library, and $450. for 16 lectures.

Mr. Elijah W. Upton presented this year two handsomely framed paintings, of President Harrison, by a native artist, Abel Nichols to whom Mr. Harrison sat in 840; also the portrait of Genl. Gideon Foster painted by Mr. Osgood of Salem. The Rules and Regulations were printed this year with the Annual Reports.

7th. Annual Report,
(1858 – 1859.)

The new Rules and Regulations for the government of the Trustees were printed in the Report this year, in which the duties of the Lyceum & Literary Committee are defined

      6409 volumes in Library.

The 16 lectures commenced 16 November 1858 and terminated 1 March 1859.

    This year Mrs. Elijah W. Upton presented two handsomely framed paintings, one of President Harrison, by a native artist Mr. Abel Nichols, to whom Mr. Harrison sat in 1840; also one of General Gideon Foster of Danvers (now Peabody), painted by Mr. Osgood of Salem.

8th. Annual Report,
(1859-1860.)

Mr. Elijah W. Upton presented the portrait of a former townsman, Rufus Choate, who delivered the oration at the dedication services, in the Institute Building in September 1854. Mr. Choate died in 1859. This painting was by Joseph Ames. 7000 volumes are now in the library.

9th. Annual Report,
(1860 - 1861.)

A second furnace was this year placed in the building; and more than the usual attention was bestowed upon the grounds around the Building.

The "wear and tear" of books by borrowers is referred to by the Librarian showing proof of the popularity of the Institute.

The 5th. Supplementary Catalogue was printed.

The Chandelier was placed in Hall.

Appropriation for Lyceum and Library Committee appear to have been $1900.

10th Annual Report.
(1861 - 1862

The need of more shelf room is impressed upon the management.

The need of Alcoves, or a larger library room are spoken of; and the recommendation of submitting this matter to a competent student of the subject is made.

It is suggested also by the Library Committee that the library should be opened every day, and several other advanced ideas are expressed by the Chairman, Mrs. B. C. Perkins.

There were 14 lectures delivered during this season with an outlay upon an appropriation of $547.53

11th. Annual Report,
(1862 – 1863.)

Considerable expenditure was made for additional accommodation for in the library room, and for improvements in Hall.

Mrs. Daniels, Mr. Peabody's sister, made a donation of 160 finely bound volumes for the Branch library at Danvers.

The #7000. insurance on library and pictures, and #15000. on real estate, is to be increased.

Mr. Elijah W. Upton presents a painting of Hon. Edward Everett, by Mr. Ames (probably Joseph who painted Mr. Choate's picture), of Boston, a companion to the one of. Rufus Choate, which was also presented by Mrs. Upton.

1842. Annual Reports, (continued)
(1860 — 1861.)

Mr. Peabody's magnificent gift of
$750.000. for the benefit of the poor
of London, having been recognized,
inpart by the bestowal upon him
of the "Freedom of the City" with much
ceremony, he consigned the beautiful
gold box in which the same was presented and the illuminated parch-
ments, with a deed of gift of the same,
to the Institute to be permanently kept
and preserved by it.

Needs of more shelf room, and better
Catalogue, are referred to.

12th. Annual Report,
(1863 - 1864.)

Considerable outlay was made upon the
rented buildings for their preservation
and to secure for them good tenants.
Also improvements in Hall and Library
were spoken of in the reports.

1 January 1864, Mr. Peabody gave 2142
volumes, 2/3 to the Peabody Institute and
1/3 to the Danvers Branch. These
were divided by the two librarians,
as the report says, "amicably and
satisfactorily."

Two framed "testimonials," presented to Mr.
Peabody in recognition of his noble gift
to the City of London, one from the Vestry
of the Parish of Chelsea (part of London),
and the other from the authorities of
London, were presented to the
Institute.

Thomas Hardy, Esq., a native and
former resident of the town, presented a
pair of Elk horns, and various mineral
specimens.

10000. volumes are now in the library,
and it is stated that there is ample shelf
room for future growth.

13 lectures were given during the year.

13th. Annual Report.
(1864 – 1865.)

The need of a new Catalogue is again impressed upon the management by the Lyceum & Library Committee.

Ten lectures were given; and this report says ~~as well as some of~~ that, except in stormy weather, ~~the~~ upon the evenings when lectures were given the steps, gateway and sidewalk in front of the building were filled with people awaiting the opening of the entrance door. The Hall in every part, even the rostrum, has been almost literally crammed, and many were obliged to return home.

A new clock was placed in the Library room. ~~which has~~

14th. Annual Report,
(1865 – 1866.)

Eight lectures given, being less than
usual of intellectual entertainment,
occasioned by a larger sum of
money, than usual, being expended in
repairs and improvements.

3500 volumes were received from Mr.
Peabody, 2/3 for the Institute & 1/3 for
the Danvers Branch.

Upon the day when his townsmen
in the United States were celebrating
Mr. Peabody's birthday, the news
was received that he had given an
additional $500,000. for the benefit
of the London poor.

The death of Hon. Robert S. Daniels occurred this year. He was constantly
identified with the work of the
Institute from its founding in 1852
until very near the time of his death.

Mr. Peabody gave 924 volumes.

$421. was expended for books, and
$286. for lectures.

A desire to have the library open each
day of the week, except Sunday, is referred
to, but the necessary expence could
prevented.

15th. Annual Report.
(1866 – 1867.)

Early in the year it was learned that
Mr. Peabody was about to re-visit this
country, and, upon motion of the Trustees
a Town Meeting was called and a Committee was appointed to go to New
York to greet him and invite him
to visit the Town and partake of its
hospitalities. He cordially received
the Committee but positively declined
any public reception, but expressed
his intention of visiting the Peabody
Institute at South Danvers upon business.

Upon a July morning Mr. Peabody
appeared at the Institute, and his business
proved to be a proposition to donate
One Hundred Thousand dollars to put
the Institute upon a basis to carry out
his original design in its foundation,
"the spread of Knowledge and morality"
among the people of his native town.

At the same time Mr. Peabody gave $40,000.
to the Danvers Branch, and arranged
for the entire separation of this Branch
from the Institute at Peabody. South Danvers
(now Peabody).

His views and desires as to the management of the
Institute are most forcibly expressed in his letter of 22 Sept.
1866, printed with the Report for this year page 13.

DSS.

1512 – continued.

In regard to his gift of the portrait of
~~his majesty~~ Queen Victoria, I will quote
what Mr. Peabody says in his letter just referred
to.

"I have only one other suggestion to make –
Her Majesty, ~~the~~ Queen Victoria, has been
pleased to do me the signal honor of
writing me a highly complimentary letter
with her own hand, and tendering me
the gift of her portrait. This is now
being executed in enamel on plate of gold
by her Majesty's artist at London, and
will be forwarded to me during the present
year. As a work of art it will be ex-
traordinary and unique: its intrinsic
value will be great, and as an unde-
served and too flattering personal testimo-
nial and tribute, its worth to me and
mine will be beyond price. Of this
letter of the Queen, her portrait, the gold
boxes from the City of London, and other
valued testimonials, I propose to make
you and your successors the custodians."

Under date of 15 October 1866, Mrs. Eliza
Sutton, having received from Mr. Peabody
a kind and cordial approval of her plan,
presented $20000. to the Institute as a
permanent fund, to be called the Eben
Dale Sutton Fund, the income as it

15th. continued.

accrues, to be devoted exclusively to the
establishment of a Reference Library;
that the books purchased for it shall be
of enduring value, and such only as
are desirable and indispensable for the
use of scholars; that they shall be
substantially and as far as practicable,
uniformly bound, and shall be kept
together in some room of the Institute
Building, especially assigned for this
accommodation, from which they shall
never be loaned or taken."

11854 Volumes now in library.

16th. Annual Report.
(1867 – 1868.)

Reconstruction and enlargement of Lecture Hall finished; internally Library room enlargement, Sutton Reference Library room, and Strong Room to contain Queen's picture and other valuables, nearly completed.

The portico to front of building has been added.

Cost of entire reconstruction and enlargement, now nearly completed for about £45 000.

The architect was Mr. G. J. F. Bryant, of Boston.

Mr. Peabody gave on 5 August 1867 £2000. to establish the High School Medal Fund.

17th. Annual Report,
(1868 – 1869.)

This year the Strong Room was put into use.

The gold medal, ordered by the Congress of the United States, and presented during the past year by the President to Mr. Peabody, in recognition of his great acts of benevolence in giving ~~a sum exceeding~~ $2 000 000. for the promotion of education in the States of the South desolated and impoverished by war.

During the year Mr. Peabody added $500 000. to his Fund for the benefit of the poor of London.

Mr. Sutton finished, fitted up and furnished the apartment provided for the Reference library.

Mr Mayall of London gave two large steel engravings of Ancient and Modern Jerusalem.

The Lyceum and Library Committee expresses doubt as to the propriety of having free-concerts; and the Trustees' report speaks strongly against them. The proposition to keep the library open any secular day and closing early in the evening, except Saturday, is referred to.

17th — continued.

A list of testimonials conferred upon
Mr. Peabody is given in the Librarian's
report for this year.

18th. Annual Report,
(1869-1870)

This year Mr. Peabody returned to his native Country; the Banquet given by him to his friends, at the Institute; and his donation of $000. to the Institute funds, ~~He returned to England, his ~~ , followed his death ~~ ~~ in a letter from him dated at Salem, 13 September 1869, and inserted on pages 11 & 12 of this year's report.

Mr. Peabody there writes: " This sum is added the funds already in the hands of your Board Trustees, and used for the purpose of the Institute already defined and stated to you in previous term, the injunctions contained in which I confirm and repeat, in every respect I trust that this sum, in addition to the funds ready at your disposal, and making in all amount of Two Hundred Thousand dollars, may make your Institute not only "independent, & wealthy, and that it may serve to large even more widely the field of usefulness, all generations, in which the Institute has ready commenced so successful a mission. "

See Mr. Peabody's note on page 13 Fifteenth Annual Report of

this same year occurred his final sickness, death obsequies at Westminster Abbey, the mausoleum of Great Britain's historic dead, where remains temporarily rested, and whence were transported, with most distinguished

1872. Continued

international honors to the home of his
youth, ending with the impressive and
elaborate funeral ceremonies in his
native Country and Town.

Mr. Peabody died November 4th 1869; and
was buried .... in the family lot
at Harmony Grove Cemetery.

General Fund amounts to # 130 000.
Eben Dale Sutton Ref: Library Fund..., 20 000.
Peabody High School Medal Fund ... 2000.

Miss. Mary J. Floyd was this year elected
librarian of the Eben Dale Sutton Reference
Library.

The North Ante-room was arranged for a Reading-room, and that with the Trustees were fitted up with the present furniture and closets.

The Treasurer includes this year, in his report, an account of the Inauguration of the "Reserved Fund Account" as follows:

"Our last interview, gentlemen, with Mr. Peabody has been most graphically described in our last Report to the Town, and on our Records of March 1870, with the resolutions resulting therefrom; both of which documents were from the successful thought and happy pen of our President, and therefore in illustrating the accounts which I herewith annex I have only to observe in substance that, at that impressive interview, on the 14th of September, A.D. 1869, of Mr. Peabody with the Trustees, met together in the Trustees' room by his individual desire, in serious and solemn consultation with them, he after carefully inspecting the ~~status and solemn consultation with, he, after carefully~~ status of the accounts and funds of the Institution, and promptly deciding upon the suggestions made to him, requested, and in so earnest a manner that the Trustees could receive it in no other form, even if they would, than an authoritative dictation, viz: That a sufficient specific portion of the funds should be set apart to accumulate in perpetuam for the purpose preserving the "Peabody Institute" to future generations, so long and so far human foresight and judgement would provide.

Agreeably to this direction of Mr. Peabody, #20 000. was set apart as a Reserved Fund, the interest of which, as it accrues, shall be added to and become a part of the principal; "no draft shall at any time be made upon this fund for the ordinary expenses of the Institute, but that it shall be allowed to increase, without deduction or interruption, until such time as it may shall be necessary to erect new edifices, or make some organic change in, or permanent addition to, the Institute, or until some great emergency shall arise, and that, then, only the accumulations shall be drawn upon and used, but that the original fund of #20 000. shall be always and forever kept whole and intact."

The foregoing extracts are from a Vote passed during 1869 – 1870, agreeably to Mr. Peabody's direction, which vote is signed by the Trustees then holding office.

20th Annual Report,
(1871-1872.)

$1700. was appropriated for a new
Catalogue, which necessitated the
closing of the library for nearly four months.

Upon consultation with Mr. C. A. Cutter,
librarian of the Boston Athenaeum, the services
of Miss. H. P. Appleton were obtained to
Superintend and carry out the re-arrang-
ing and re-cataloguing. Her Experience
in the Athenaeum, and at the Springfield
Public Library, eminently fitted her for
this work.

21st. Annual Report,
(1872 – 1873.)

The Hammond House was purchased for the Reserve Fund.

The library sustained a severe loss by the death of the librarian Mr Fitch Poole.

Mr. Theodore M. Osborn was elected his successor, and entered upon the work 1 October 1873.

It being is proposed in the similar report to contain a well ventilated Reading - room.

22nd. Annual Report,
(1873 – 1874.)

~~Nothing especial to note.~~
The affairs of the Institute are favorably reported upon

23d. Annual Report,
(1874 – 1875.)

The beautiful and valuable set of
Audubon's Birds was presented by
Mrs. Sutton to the Reference Library.
The question of what shall be
the character of the lectures seems
to have been again been under
consideration.   Ten lectures were
given, and The Committee say the attendance has been
large, and they consider the course successful.
Reserved Fund   amounts to   # 26 599. 94
Permanent Fund   "   "   112 250. 00
High School Medal Fund   "   "   2 000. 00
E. D. Sutton Fund   "   "   20 000. 00
                                  _____
                              #   159 847. 94

24th. Annual Report,
(1875–1876.)

In the Trustees report reference is made to the fact that medical works constitute a large part of the additions to the Sutton Library. These are works of great value and too expensive for ordinary purchase by physicians. The convenient access to them, here, cannot fail to be of great advantage to the Town in general, as well as to the individuals consulting them.

This is the Centennial year of our Country (1876), and also ~~marks~~ is the twentieth year since our first Catalogue was printed.

25th. Annual Report,
(1876 – 1877.)

The Hall is to be somewhat changed before another Lecture Season, so that more ample means of speedy Egress will be secured to audiences, and the doors will be hung on hinges swinging both ways.

The need of a reading-room in connection with the library is spoken of by the Lyceum and Library Committee, and the Trustees' report says that it will be provided as soon as possible.

Mr. Sutton's generous gifts of books are continually enlarging the Reference Library, and increasing its usefulness.

The following vote was passed to meet a question that came before them :- Voted, That it is not prudent or proper that the hall of the Institute should be used for theatrical or dramatic entertainments, or for any purpose which will endanger the recovery of endurance on our policies in case of loss by fire; and that the Board of Trustees will cordially sustain the Committee on Buildings in such a policy in regard to the general use of the hall as their Committee shall deem most promotive of the objects and purposes of the Founder of the Institute.

Reserved Fund now amounts to   ⁑ 29 929.77
Permanent Fund   „   „   „   117 750.00
Eben Dale Sutton Library Fund.   „   „   20 000.00
Peabody High School Medal Fund „   „   2 000.00
  ⁑ 169 679.77

The copy of the "Milton Shield" presented by Mrs. Sutton. The original shield,

26th. continued.

of which this is a fac simile, was made for the Paris Exhibition in 1867, and is the unaided work of Morel Ladœuil. The subjects selected for illustration on the shield are taken from Milton's "Paradise Lost", sixth book.

There are now 18500 volumes on the shelves.

A list of past and present officers was issued with the Annual Reports of this year.

By the Will of the late Eben S. Osborn, dated May 30, 1877, with Edward W. Jacobs and D. Webster King, legal Trustees of half the property, Executors and administrators, (Mrs. Eliza Sutton and the Trustees of the Institute agreeing that the Trustees under the Will may be exempt from giving sureties on their bonds as Trustees of said funds) the Sutton Library of Peabody, Mass. is to receive said half of the property upon the death of his widow.

27th. Annual Report,
(1878 – 1879.)

The affairs of the Institute are
favorably reported upon.

28th. Annual Report,
(1879-1880.)

The income of the Permanent Fund for the year is given as $7661.50.

Estimated cost of Books in the Library is given at $60.000.

The Trustees voted to accept the custody of the Gold Medal and Diploma awarded to the Trustees of the Peabody Educational Fund at the Paris Exposition of 1878, and that they "will carefully treasure and hold the same subject to the order of the said Educational Fund Trustees".

Mr. Thomas M Stimpson, for many years the valued and efficient head of the Lyceum and Library Committee urges the importance of ample endowance on the Peabody Library.

Mr. Wm. F. Poole of Chicago is quoted as saying "a reading-room is a necessary adjunct to a Public Library", and this Report adds that this is the greatest need of the Institute.

29th. Annual Report,
(1880 – 1881)

$500. was appropriated for the purpose
of instituting a Reading-room in the
Library Hall.

The death of John H. Teague, the faith-
ful retired Janitor, occurred December
4th, 1880; and John D. McKeen was
appointed to succeed him.

In the fall of 1880 Mrs. Theodore M.
Osborne, who had been librarian for nearly
eight years, tendered his resignation, and
Mrs. J. Warren Upton was appointed to fill
the vacancy.

Mr. Sutton's donations of books still
continue to enlarge the Reference library.

Considerable work has been done upon
the outside of the Institute Building and
the dwelling houses, as well as on the
iron fencing and the stone posts in
front of the main entrance to Building.

Eben Dale Sutton Library has now 1900
volumes; and it is stated that the
purchased books have cost $9500..
Mrs. Sutton's gifts of books amount to
several thousands more.

30th Annual Report,
(1881-1882.)

The reduced income, lessened by the lower rates of interest, is referred to in the Report.

$70000. of the funds were loaned to the Town at 6¾ per cent; but when the notes matured the agents of the Town refused to pay a higher rate than that at which the loan could be readily negotiated in the open market. The new rate is fixed at 4%. It is stated that some towns have, under similar circumstances, continued such loans at the former rates of interest in aid of the beneficial influence of a public library.

The new rates lowers the income $1500. The writer of the Trustees Report refers to the decided instructions to the Trustees contained in Mr Peabody's letters of gift, and also given by him personally at his meeting with the Trustees in the Institute during his last visit to the Country.

36th. Annual Report,
(1882 – 1883.)

A change in the hour of Keeping the library open was made this year, and it is now open as follows: — Mondays from 2 to 8; Wednesdays and Saturdays from 2 to 9; and Thursdays from 2 to 6 P.m.

The whole number of volumes in the library, not including a large number of volumes of U.S. and Mass. Public documents not catalogued, and 175 Volumes of the new series of the U.S. Patent office Reports, is 23271.

The librarian ~~Mr. J. Warren Upton~~ gives several tables, in connection with the library work, which are of interest

3 2nd Annual Report,
(1883 – 1884.)

The relative authority of the Board of
Trustees and of the Lyceum and Library
Committee is considered by the writer of
this Report, and various opinions upon
the subject are expressed.

The Reserved Fund, and its purpose, is
also considered.

The Chairman of the Lyceum and
Library Committee writes at length
upon the future needs and possibilities
of the constantly increasing library.
He speaks of the need of a separate
reading room being felt, and says that
it is possible that, if the Town Hall can
be used in the future for Lectures, any
question of new buildings, or any costly
additions to the present one, might be
postponed many years, if it ever be-
comes necessary to deal with it.

He raises the question whether a portion
of the income of the Reserved Fund cannot
rightly be spared for yearly library
Expenses. The L. & L. Committee report is, by
Mr. Stimpson and, of interest.

The Town Hall was used this year for
the first time for the delivery of the free lectures
and this new plan is well spoken of by Mr.
Stimpson.

The Chairman of the Peabody Library Committee, Mr. S. Endicott says among other things in his report: "For such a library as this, more attention ought to be paid to the permanent value of books than to their immediate popularity, or the demand for them on their publication. It is the function of a public library to furnish to the citizens the means of making exact and thorough acquisitions of knowledge in all branches of history, biography, science, art and literature; and every valuable book may be the source of benefit through scores of years to come, which cannot easily be measured or calculated."

33d. Annual Report,
(1884 – 1885.)

Hon. Alfred A. Abbott, President of the Board of Trustees and a ~~constant~~ but member of the Board since ~~its~~ 1858, ~~from foundation~~ ~~first formed~~, a friend of Mr. Peabody * and one who advised with him when Mr. Peabody established this beneficent Institution, died in October 1884.

The Board upon the day of his funeral, October 30th, passed appropriate resolutions and adjourned to attend the funeral in a body.

The Institute Building was closed to the public during the day of the funeral.

34th. Annual Report,
(1885 – 1886.)

#4400. was appropriated for the
use of the Lyceum and Library Committee.

This year the Trustees had all the oil
paintings examined by a competent
and skillful artist from Boston, who put
them into the best of order, which has
brought back the original colors.

A list of young-folks books has been
carefully prepared by the librarian for
use at the public schools, so that reading
matter can be easily selected by the teachers
for their pupils.

The means for preserving what now exists
of a card catalogue is much needed.

Number of volumes now in library,
1 February 1886, is 25507.

35th. Annual Report,
(1886 – 1887.)

The Trustees this year accepted # 1000.
as a fund, the income of which is to be
used towards keeping the George Peabody of
London lot in Harmony Grove Cemetery in
good order.

The Heirs of Mr. Peabody were the givers of
this Fund, and they previously caused the
marble tablets to be renewed and reset in
an improved form, as well as to have the
stone work put into good order, and the
Sodding repaired.

In the report a quest is made
that the School Committee be authorized
to present to the Institute copies of all
books that are used in the Schools.

~~The librarian gives a list of the~~
~~been important books that are added~~
~~to the library from 1 February 1886~~

36th. Annual Report,
(1887-1888.)

A card catalogue case has ~~already~~ been placed in the Library, and work in filling it is as far advanced as has been possible.

The need of increased Catalogue facilities is strongly presented to the Trustees. It is ten years since the supplement to the original Catalogue was printed.

Since 1 June 1887 the Library has been opened to the public every week day from 2 to 8 P.m., and on Saturdays until 9: P. m.

The Report of the Lyceum Committee raises the question whether a high class of musical performances could properly be included in the Lecture course.

It may be stated that in the gift from Mr. Babcock of a grand piano is recorded in the 6th. Annual Report.

37th. Annual Report.
(1888-1889.)

The value of the "Finding List," recently
arrived from the publishers, is most
favorably spoken of.

The Finance Committee have about
completed negotiations for the Harris
Estate which adjoins the Institute grounds
on the Easterly side.

Attention is called to the fact that the
Lyceum and Library Committee have the entire
control and management of the library, also
of the lectures and entertainments the Trustees preserving
only to themselves the appointment of the
Janitor and the regulation of his salary,
limiting the Lyceum and Library Committee
only by the amount of money which they
can use; and in this respect the
office of Trustee is little more than
honorary.

Referring to the office of Trustee the
report says that, inasmuch as the Trust
is mainly a financial one, should not
citizens of the best financial ability
and standing be chosen.

In referring to the Bond required
of the Treasurer, the report seems to
suggest that the Town might in some
way assume the cost of the Bond.

The income yielding property in 1870 and 1889 was, respectively, as follows:—

	1870	1889
Real Estate and Invest.t Funds	# 110,300.00	# 121,619.10
Reserved Fund	20,000.00	43,075.73
E.D.S. Library Fund	20,000.00	20,000.00
High School Medal Fund	2,000.00	2,269.00
Burial Lot Fund		1,000.00
Totals	# 152,300.00	# 187,963.83

Insurance.

	1875	1889
Institute Building	# 25,000.00	# 25,000.00
Library	9,500.00	20,000.00
Portraits &c.	1,550.00	
Piano & furniture.	300.00	} 1,850.00
Wallis house.		3,000.00
Merrill "	} 5,000.00	2,000.00
Hammond "	1,000.00	1,000.00
Sutton library fixtures.	5,000.00	5,000.00
Sutton Library.	2,000.00	7,000.00
Totals	# 49,350.00	# 64,850.00

www.ingramcontent.com/pod-product-compliance
Lightning Source LLC
Chambersburg PA
CBHW031747090426
42739CB00008B/910